COSENTINO

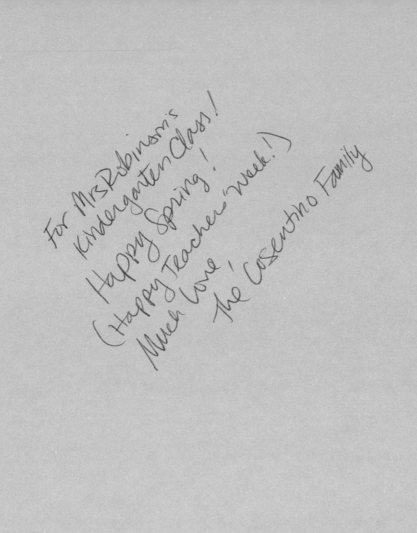

For Mrs Robinson's
Kindergarten Class!
Happy Spring!
(Happy Teacher week!)
Much Love,
The Cosentino Family

Summer Birds

The Butterflies of Maria Merian

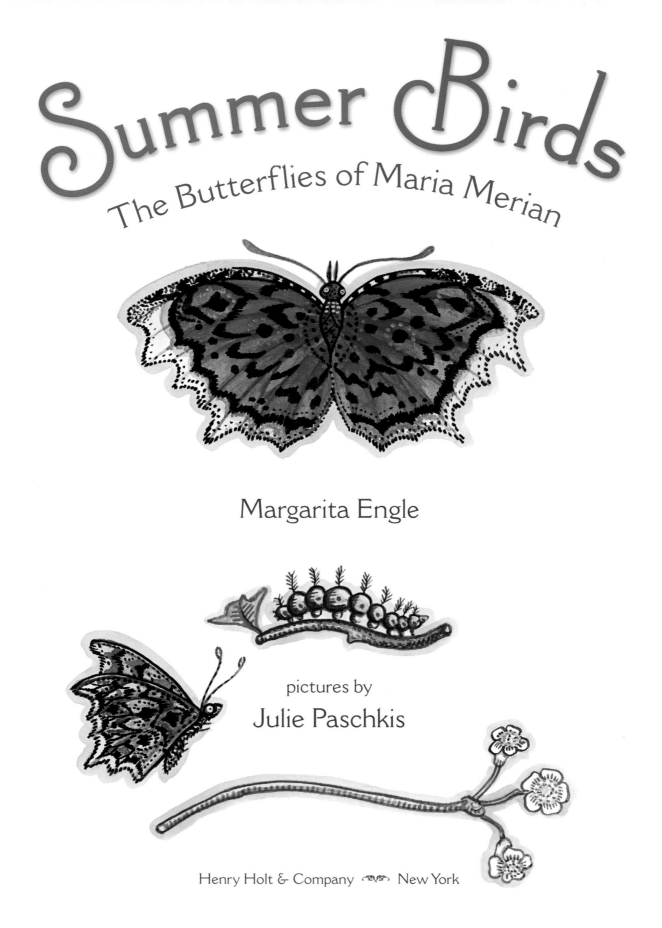

Margarita Engle

pictures by
Julie Paschkis

Henry Holt & Company ❧ New York

For Curtis Engle and Lynn LeBeck and Marshall W. Johnson,
my favorite entomologists, and for my sister Madalyn, who filled
our room with butterflies and caterpillars when we were little
—M. E.

For Zoe Paschkis, scientist and artist
—J. P.

I thank God for summer birds, scientists, and artists. I am deeply grateful to
my family, and to Julie Paschkis for brilliant illustrations, and to Reka Simonsen for
the gift of editing. I am also grateful to Robin Tordini, Tim Jones, and everyone
else at Henry Holt and Company. Special thanks to the Special Collections and
Archives, UCR Libraries, University of California–Riverside.

Henry Holt and Company, LLC
Publishers since 1866
175 Fifth Avenue, New York
New York 10010
mackids.com

Library of Congress Cataloging-in-Publication Data
Engle, Margarita.
Summer birds : the butterflies of Maria Merian / by Margarita Engle:
illustrations by Julie Paschkis. — 1st ed.
p. cm.
ISBN 978-0-8050-8937-0
1. Caterpillars—Juvenile literature.
2. Butterflies—Metamorphosis—Juvenile literature.
3. Merian, Maria Sibylla, 1647–1717—Juvenile literature.
I. Paschkis, Julie, ill. II. Title.
QL544.2.E54 2010   595.78'139—dc22   2009005267

First Edition—2010
Book designed by Linda Lockowitz
Printed in China by Macmillan Production Asia Ltd.,
Kwun Tong, Kowloon, Hong Kong (Supplier Code: 10)

3 5 7 9 10 8 6 4

"Summer birds" was a medieval name
for the mysterious butterflies and moths
that appeared suddenly during warm
weather and vanished in the fall.

Each year, the sky fills with summer birds. Many people call them butterflies. Everyone believes that these insects come from mud, as if by magic.

I disagree. I am only thirteen years old, but I capture insects. I study them.

I have to catch my insects in secret.
Neighbors would accuse me
of witchcraft if they knew.

Everyone says insects are evil,
but I know my summer birds
are beautiful and harmless.

I keep caterpillars and summer birds in boxes
and jars. I feed the caterpillars with leaves.

I sit still. I watch.

Caterpillars are born
from eggs laid by
summer birds.
(butterflies)

The caterpillars eat leaves,
and they grow and eat
some more.

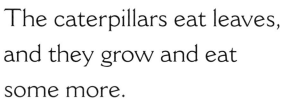

When the caterpillars
are big enough, they
spin cocoons. These are
made of silky threads.

While the caterpillars rest
inside their silky cocoons,
they turn into
summer birds.
(butterflies)

The summer birds come out of their
cocoons with wings, ready to fly.

Then they fly from one flower to another,
sipping nectar.

I know the grown-ups are wrong about summer birds.
Insects are not born from mud.

I have seen their whole life cycle with my own eyes.
Insects grow slowly, changing from one form to
another. None of the forms are evil.

I love to paint colorful pictures of every kind
of caterpillar, cocoon, and summer bird.
I keep a notebook filled with my paintings.
I write down everything the summer birds do.

In my paintings, I always show

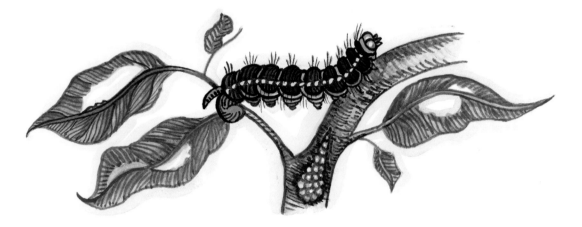

which kinds of leaves the caterpillars eat.

I also paint the flowers where summer birds drink nectar.

Sometimes I think that I am like a summer bird, waiting to fly. Right now, I am a child, but in a few years, I will be grown. When I am a grown-up, I will be free to travel to faraway lands, painting all sorts of rare summer birds and flowers.

Maybe I will even paint the lizards and frogs of faraway lands.

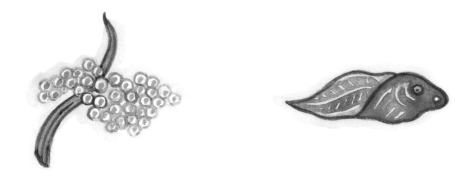

I have some tadpoles in a jar of water. I have seen how they are born from eggs, not from mud.

I watch the tadpoles eat and grow, until finally, when they are big enough, they begin to grow legs.

The tadpoles have turned into frogs.

Someday, I will put my paintings into a book. Then everyone will know the truth about small animals that change their forms.

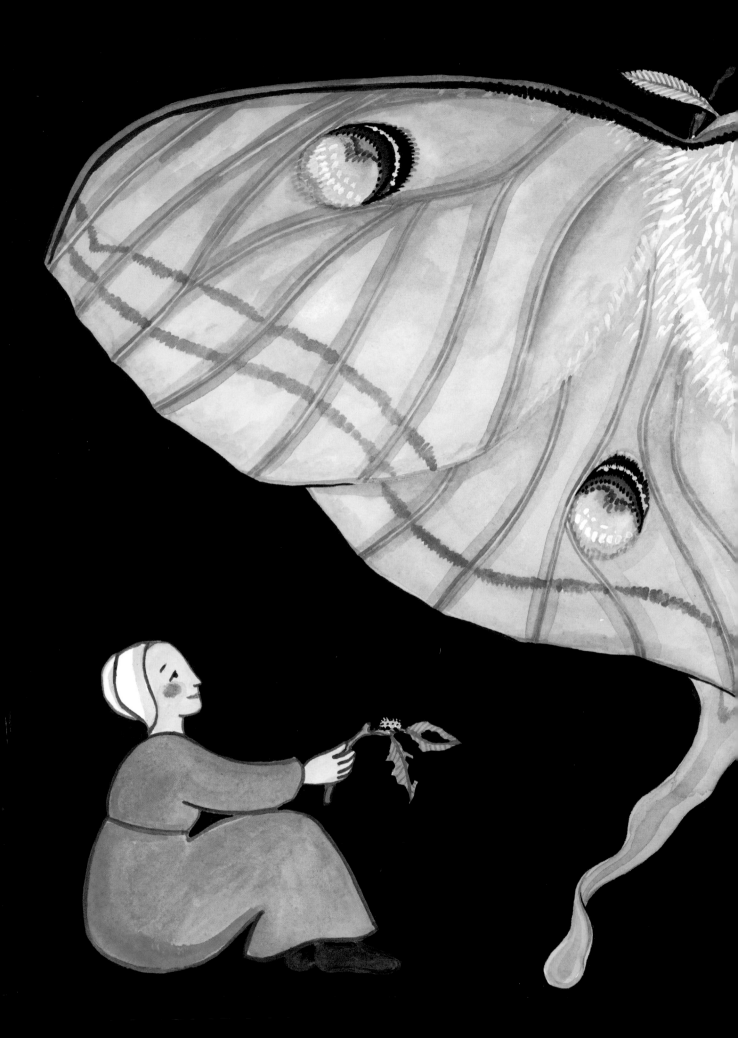

When people understand the life
cycles of creatures that change forms,
they will stop calling small animals evil.
They will learn, as I have, by seeing
a wingless caterpillar turn into a
flying summer bird.

Historical Note

Maria Sibylla Merian was born in Frankfurt, Germany, in 1647. When she was only three, she already displayed such enthusiasm for painting that her father, an engraver, predicted she would become a great artist. After her father's death, her mother remarried a painter who encouraged Maria's interest in flowers and insects.

Maria's curiosity about small living things was unusual at the time, because Europeans still believed that beetles, worms, larvae, caterpillars, and frogs were formed from mud. This idea of "spontaneous generation" from a nonliving puddle of wet dirt was an ancient Greek concept that led Europeans to think of insects and other small creatures as "beasts of the devil." People feared the natural process of metamorphosis, or changing forms, from caterpillar to butterfly or from tadpole to frog. If animals could "shape shift," then couldn't people also be transformed into werewolves and other fearsome beasts?

At the age of thirteen, Maria was already well on her way to disproving the ancient theory. By careful observation, she discovered that metamorphosis is natural, not supernatural. There was no witchcraft involved and nothing to fear. Beginning with silkworms brought from Asia by a merchant, she watched the slow process of change, recording every detail in her notes and sketches. Her studies were far ahead of her time.

She eventually became famous as a scientist, an artist, and an explorer. At a time when women rarely traveled at all, she and her younger daughter, Dorothea, went to South America alone. In Suriname, she painted insects, plants, birds, and reptiles. Just as she'd hoped, Maria's paintings were published in beautiful books that helped people understand the life cycles of flowers and insects. Her work was admired and collected by Russia's czar Peter the Great. Today, as a result of Maria Sibylla Merian's careful studies, we know that butterflies, moths, and frogs do not spring from mud. We also know that they are not evil, but natural and amazing.